Contents

D0815256

COUNTING DOWN THE HUMAN BODY

The human body is made up of external and internal organs. The external organs are everything that you can see on your body, such as your skin, nose, and ears. The internal organs are underneath your skin and include your heart, lungs, and brain.

EXTERNAL ORGANS

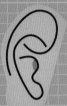

INTERNAL ORGANS

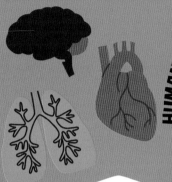

HUMAN TISSUE UNDER THE MICROSCOPE

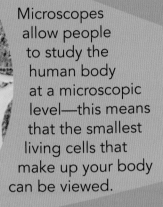

Microscopes allow people to study the human body at a microscopic level—this means that the smallest living cells that make up your body can be viewed.

ANATOMY

The study of the human body in science is known as anatomy. The study of anatomy dates back to the ancient Egyptians around **1600 BC**, when they showed an understanding of how the heart operates, possibly through the practice of human sacrifice.

To understand how the inside of the body works, the body had to be dissected. This means that the body was cut open to reveal what was inside.

Just beneath the skin, there is a complex system of muscles. Learn more about your muscles on pages 18–19.

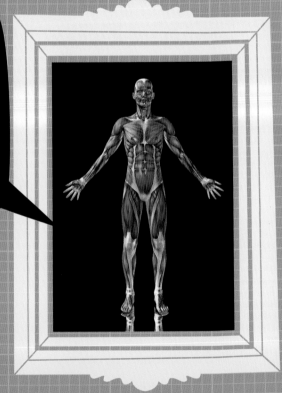

GROWING AND AGING

Throughout your life your body continues to change. The body reaches full growth at around age **21**. After that, your body still develops but it will not experience the same level of growth. For example, you will not grow any taller. From this point on, the body starts an aging process whereby the body is slower at repairing itself. Later in life, the body will also begin to shrink. You will lose at least **0.4 inches** (1 cm) in height every decade after age **40**. By **80**, most men will be **2 inches** (5 cm) shorter and women **3 inches** (8 cm) shorter than they were in their **twenties**.

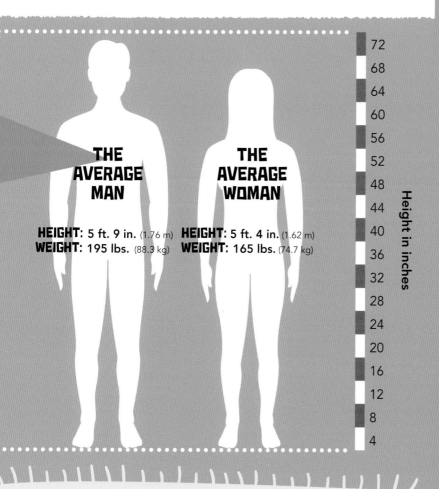

THE AVERAGE MAN
HEIGHT: 5 ft. 9 in. (1.76 m)
WEIGHT: 195 lbs. (88.3 kg)

THE AVERAGE WOMAN
HEIGHT: 5 ft. 4 in. (1.62 m)
WEIGHT: 165 lbs. (74.7 kg)

Height in inches

72
68
64
60
56
52
48
44
40
36
32
28
24
20
16
12
8
4

EVERYBODY'S BODY IS DIFFERENT

Bodies are different in shape, color, the amount of hair they have, and sometimes even in the number of fingers and toes they have. When talking about the human body, scientists will often refer to an average measurement to use as an example. This average was determined by studying many bodies, calculating the most common size that seems best to represent the majority of human bodies.

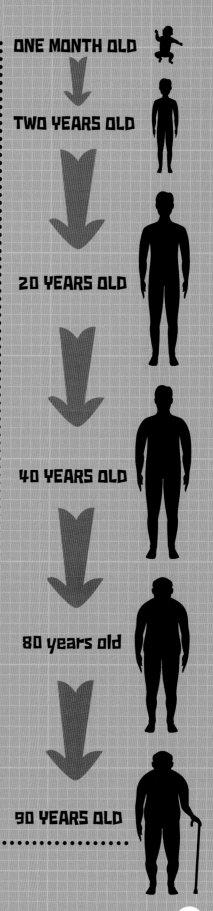

ONE MONTH OLD

TWO YEARS OLD

20 YEARS OLD

40 YEARS OLD

80 years old

90 YEARS OLD

THERE ARE 100 TRILLION GOOD BACTERIA LIVING IN THE HUMAN BODY

Bacteria are life forms. Many types of bacteria exist as single cells that live in the air, the ground, and in all living things, including humans.

GOOD AND BAD BACTERIA

The human body comes into contact with both good and bad bacteria every day. Good bacteria help you to digest your food, create some of the vitamins your body needs, and protect you from bad bacteria.

Bad bacteria can be the cause of many infections. Common bacterial infections are those that affect the eyes, throat, or skin. Bad bacteria can also cause food poisoning, meningitis, and pneumonia. Fortunately, there are more good bacteria in your body than bad, and the good bacteria feed off the bad bacteria.

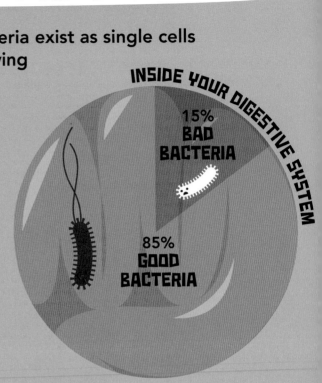

INSIDE YOUR DIGESTIVE SYSTEM

15% BAD BACTERIA

85% GOOD BACTERIA

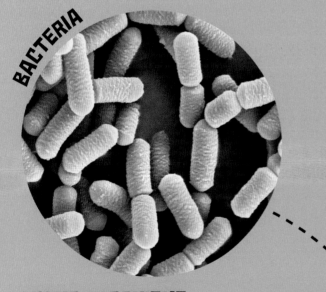

BACTERIA

It takes **1,000,000,000 bacterial cells** to cover a pinhead.

The largest bacterial cells are only **0.0004 inches** (0.01 mm) long!

LIVING ORGANISMS

Bacteria are a form of microorganism—this means that they are so small, they can only be seen through a powerful microscope. Bacteria are living organisms, but they are not built like animals or even the tiniest of insects; bacteria have a cell-like structure.

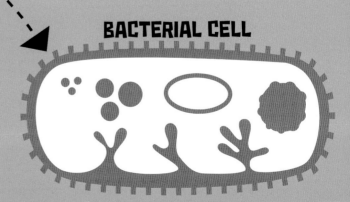

BACTERIAL CELL

BACTERIAL CELLS ARE EVERYWHERE

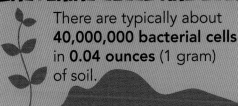

There are typically about **40,000,000 bacterial cells** in **0.04 ounces** (1 gram) of soil.

There are about **1,000,000 bacterial cells** in **0.03 ounces** (1 ml) of fresh water.

Bacteria multiply in warm conditions with plenty of food and water; this includes living off the liquids and foods that pass through your body. **Bacteria can divide into two every 20 minutes.**

Number of minutes	Bacterial cells
20	
40	
60	
80	
100	
120	

After **six hours, one bacterium** could become **131,072 bacteria**.

There are more bacterial cells in your body than human cells. Bacterial cells outnumber human cells by a factor of **ten to one**. We are more bacteria than we are human!

WHERE?

Bacteria live all over the outside and inside of your body.

Some scientists believe that there may be **10,000,000,000,000** (10 trillion) **bacterial cells** in the human digestive system, whereas others believe there could be as many as **100,000,000,000,000** (100 trillion)! The majority of bacteria can be found in the intestines, where they help digest food.

THERE ARE APPROXIMATELY:

6,000,000,000 bacterial cells in your mouth. That's over **four times** the population of China.

7,000,000 bacterial cells on your arms. That's equivalent to having the population of Hong Kong crawling all over your arms.

3,000,000 bacterial cells on your armpits. That's the population of Chicago in your armpits.

500,000 bacterial cells on your hands. That's the population of Sacramento, California, on your hands.

THERE ARE ONE TRILLION, 300 BILLION SKIN CELLS ON THE HUMAN BODY

Skin is the largest organ of the human body. It holds all your other organs together, protects your bones, muscles, and internal organs, allows you to feel and react to heat and cold. It is a huge sensor containing nerves that tell the brain what is going on around your body.

THE FUNCTIONS OF SKIN

Produces oils that act as a waterproof raincoat

Protects you from the sun's UV rays

Keeps moisture inside the body

Regulates your body temperature

Cushions your body from strong blows

Defends your body against harmful bacteria

Skin is made up of layers of cells. There are approximately **1,300,000,000 skin cells** on the human body. Every minute you lose between **30,000 to 40,000 dead skin cells**, which are replaced by new ones. Almost all of your skin is replaced every month.

There are **22 sq. ft.** (2 sq. meters) of skin covering the average human body. That's the size of a double bed sheet.

More than **50% of dust** in your home is actually dead skin.

0.002 inches (0.05 mm) thick

The thinnest area of skin on your body is on your eyelids.

0.06 inches (1.5 mm) thick

The thickest area of skin is found on the soles of your feet.

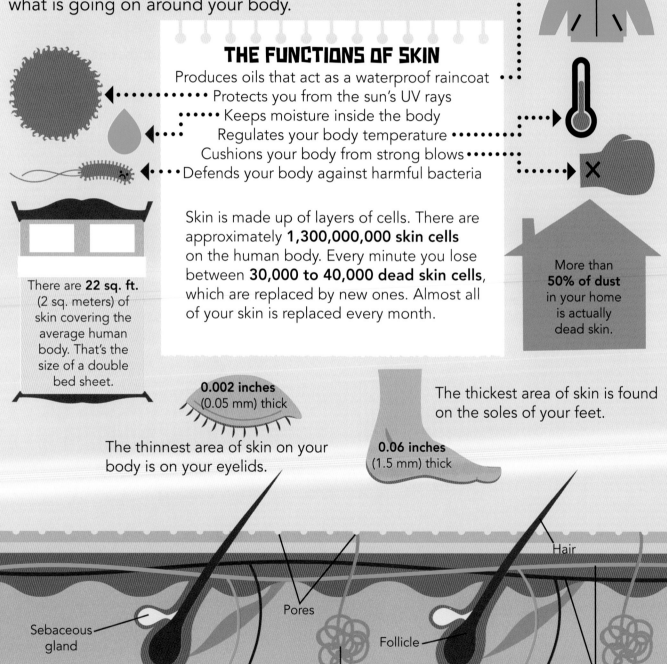

Hair

Pores

Sebaceous gland

Follicle

Blood vessels

Sweat gland

SKIN COLOR

The color of human skin depends on the amount of pigment, called melanin, a coloring substance that the body produces. Melanin also gives your eyes and hair their color. The freckles on your face are also patches of melanin. Small amounts of melanin result in light skin, while large amounts result in dark skin.

PIMPLES

Pimples, also known as acne, are caused by an overproduction of cells in the skin's sweat and sebaceous glands. **Eight out of 10** people between the ages of **11** and **30** will be affected by acne.

NAILS

Your fingernails and toenails are made of keratin, which is part of the epidermis layer of skin. It's the same substance in a bird's beak.

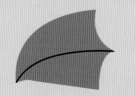

Skin has three layers

FIRST LAYER: EPIDERMIS

The epidermis is the top layer of skin. This layer acts as a waterproof barrier. Pores cover this layer, acting as an outlet for sweat that comes through the sweat glands. Hair also pokes through the surface.

SECOND LAYER: DERMIS

The dermis is the middle layer, where the hair and sweat glands begin.

THIRD LAYER: HYPODERMIS

The hypodermis is at the bottom. It is largely made of fatty tissue.

On average, fingernails grow **0.1 inches** (2.5 mm) a month. Fingernails grow **four times** faster than toenails.

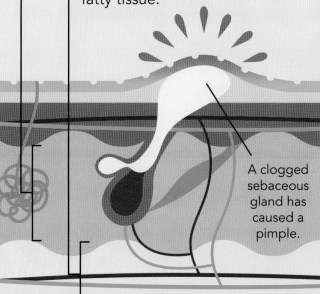

A clogged sebaceous gland has caused a pimple.

Lee Redmond

Lee Redmond holds the record for the world's longest fingernails. She had been growing them for **28 years**, and they were more than **28 feet** (8.65 m) long. That's an average growth of 1 foot (30 cm) a year. In 2009 she lost them in a car accident.

1 YEAR: 12 IN. (30 CM)

10 YEARS: 10 FT. (3 M)

20 YEARS: 20 FT. (6 M)

28 YEARS: 28 FT. (8.65 M)

BLONDS HAVE 146 THOUSAND STRANDS OF HAIR ON THEIR HEADS

Hair grows up from underneath the skin. It keeps you warm and helps to protect parts of your body.

Hair Follicles

Your head is covered with about **100,000 hair follicles**.

Your body is covered with about **5,000,000 hair follicles**.

Some of the hair on your body is easy to see, like your eyebrows and the hair on your head, arms, and legs. But other hair, like that on your cheeks, is almost invisible. Hair can cover the whole body except for the soles of the feet, palms of the hands, and lips.

Humans have about the same number of hair follicles as chimpanzees. But chimpanzees look hairier because their hair grows longer, thicker, and darker than human hair.

HAIR GROWTH

Hair grows about **0.5 inches** (12.7 mm) **per month.** It would take **10 years** to grow **5 feet** (1.524 m).

One month

One year

Five years

Ten years

If a man never shaved his beard, it would grow to about **30 feet** (9 m) in a lifetime.

30 ft. (9 m)

HAIR LOSS

You shed around **100 hairs** on your head a day. If your hair didn't regrow, you would lose all your hair in approximately **two years and nine months**.

Eyebrow hair can last between **3–5 months** before it sheds. An eyelash can have a lifespan of about **150 days**.

Day one

Eight months, one week

One year, four months, two weeks

Two years, nine months

150

The hair that we see above the skin's surface is made of dead cells, which is why it doesn't cause any pain when someone cuts your hair.

BALDNESS

People who are bald have no hair growing on their head. The cause of baldness is believed to be genetic. This means that if your parents, grandparents, or great-grandparents were bald, there is an increased chance that you will also go bald. The baldness gene is much less common in women, but as women get older, their hair tends to thin out.

Some studies show that there is a four in seven chance of receiving the baldness gene.

You can begin to go bald as early as your late teens. Approximately **25%** of men begin balding by age **30**.

As you grow older the rate of hair regrowth slows down. **66%** of men begin balding by age **60**.

HAIR COLOR

There may be an average of **100,000 strands of hair** on the human head, but the actual amount will vary depending on your hair color.

Blonds have an average of **146,000** hair strands.

People with brown hair have an average of **100,000** hair strands.

Approximately **1%** of the world's population are redheads. About **13%** of Scotland's population has red hair.

People with black hair have an average of **110,000** hair strands.

Redheads have an average of **86,000** hair strands.

THE HEART BEATS ONE HUNDRED THOUSAND TIMES A DAY

The heart is one of the body's strongest muscles.
It pumps blood to every part of your body, making sure it receives the nutrients you need. The heart is the size of a fist and on average, weighs around **11 ounces** (300 g)—the weight of **six medium-sized eggs**.

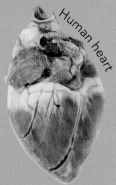

Human heart

THE HEART HAS FOUR CHAMBERS

The top two chambers are called the left atrium and right atrium. *Atrium* is Latin for "entrance hall."
The two lower chambers are called the left ventricle and the right ventricle. *Ventricle* is Latin for "little belly."
Each of the **four chambers** has a valve that makes sure the blood flows through them in **one direction**. The thumping sound of the heartbeat is the sound of the **four heart valves** closing.

The right side of the heart pumps blood to the lungs. The right atrium holds about **3.5 tablespoons** (52 ml) of blood.

The left ventricle holds just over **four tablespoons** (59 ml) of blood.

BLOOD CIRCULATION

The movement of blood is called circulation. The heart pumps more than **1,850 gallons** (7,000 liters) of blood through **60,000 miles** (96,560 km) of blood vessels each day.

A newborn baby has about **one cup of blood** (237 ml) in circulation, but within a person's lifetime, the heart will have pumped enough blood to fill **three super tankers**.

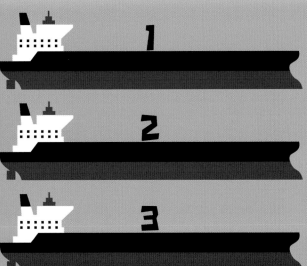

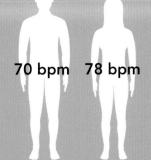

70 bpm   78 bpm

bpm = beats per minute
The heart beats to pump blood. The average heart beats **60–80 times** per minute. On average, a woman's heart beats faster than a man's.

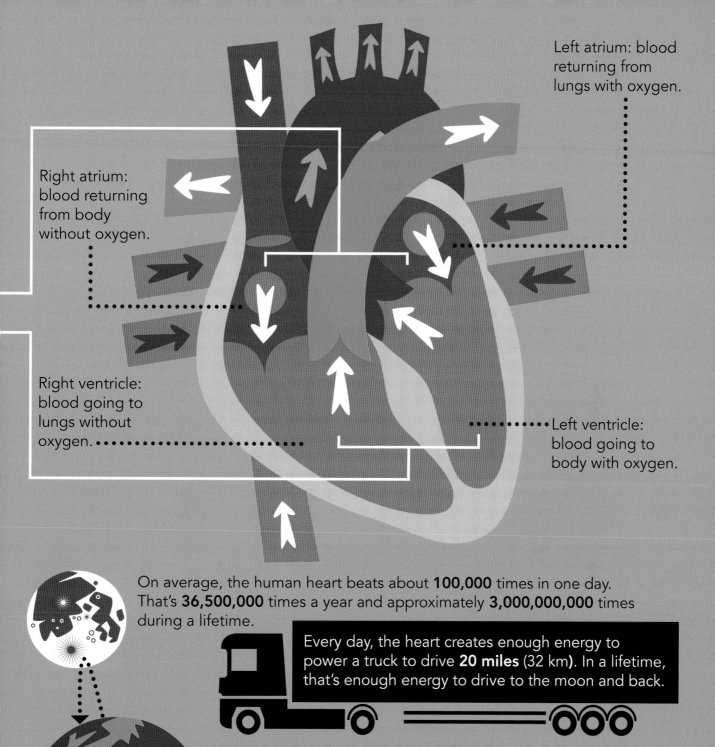

Left atrium: blood returning from lungs with oxygen.

Right atrium: blood returning from body without oxygen.

Right ventricle: blood going to lungs without oxygen.

Left ventricle: blood going to body with oxygen.

On average, the human heart beats about **100,000** times in one day. That's **36,500,000** times a year and approximately **3,000,000,000** times during a lifetime.

Every day, the heart creates enough energy to power a truck to drive **20 miles** (32 km). In a lifetime, that's enough energy to drive to the moon and back.

COUNTING YOUR HEARTBEATS

You can feel your heart beating and pumping blood around your body at areas called pulse points. One is on the inside of your wrist. Gently place two fingertips there to feel your heartbeat, or pulse.

Count the number of beats for **one minute**. If you have just been exercising, you will notice that the beats are faster.

BLOOD TRAVELS SIXTY THOUSAND MILES (96,560 KM) A DAY

Blood is a red liquid that circulates through your body. It carries oxygen and nutrients around the body and moves out waste products. Men have approximately **1.5 gallons** (5.6 liters) of blood in their bodies. Women have about **1.2 gallons** (4.5 liters) of blood in their bodies.

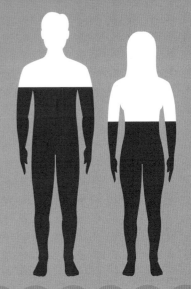

BLOOD IS MADE UP OF:

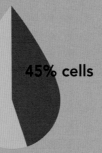

55% plasma

45% cells

Plasma is a yellow liquid in which the blood cells float. Plasma is made up of **90% water**.

THE CELLULAR COMPONENTS OF BLOOD ARE:

Red blood cells	White blood cells	Platelets

1:600

1   600

A quarter of cells in the human body are red blood cells. On average, it takes **30–45 seconds** for red blood cells to circulate around the body. They are produced at a rate of **4,000,000,000 to 5,000,000,000 every hour**.

There is **one white blood cell** for every **600 red blood cells**. White blood cells are an important part of the body's immune system. They defend against certain bacteria, viruses, and infectious diseases.

Platelets help prevent bleeding and make the blood clot when a cut is made. The blood clot enables the skin cells to grow over the wound.

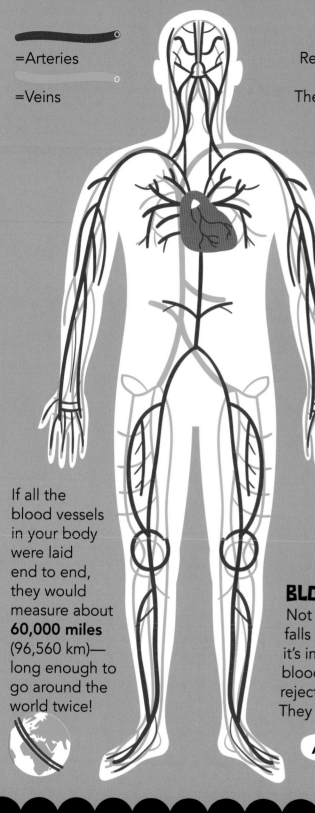

=Arteries

=Veins

BLOOD CELL LIFE SPANS

Red blood cells circulate inside the body for **120 days**.

There are different types of white blood cells, ranging in life span from **three to 20 days**.

Platelets have a life span of **three to four days**.

BLOOD VESSELS

Blood circulates around the body through a system of blood vessels. There are three main types:

- ARTERIES

These carry the oxygen-rich blood away from the heart to all of the body's tissues. They branch out and become smaller and smaller as they carry blood further from the heart.

- VEINS

These carry oxygen-poor blood back to the heart. They become larger and larger the closer they are to the heart.

- CAPILLARIES

These are small thin blood vessels that connect the arteries and veins.

If all the blood vessels in your body were laid end to end, they would measure about **60,000 miles** (96,560 km)— long enough to go around the world twice!

BLOOD TYPES

Not everyone has the same type of blood. If someone falls ill and needs new blood pumped into their body, it's important that they have blood from the same blood type as themselves, otherwise their body will reject it. There are four main types of human blood. They are categorized as:

| A | B | AB | O |

In Japan, blood types are given personality traits:

**Type A
The farmer**
Serious and trustworthy

**Type B
The hunter**
Curious, enthusiastic, and independent

**Type AB
The humanist**
Considerate and sensitive

**Type O
The warrior**
Outgoing and expressive

WE TAKE 20 THOUSAND BREATHS A DAY

When you breathe, you breathe in oxygen and breathe out carbon dioxide.

This exchange of gases takes place in the lungs. The lungs are internal organs that form part of the respiratory system—the system that enables you to breathe. Once in the lungs, oxygen passes through the lung walls into the red blood cells in nearby capillaries. The red blood cells then carry the oxygen around the body, generating the energy you need to live.

RED BLOOD CELLS CARRY OXYGEN

LUNGS

You have two lungs that sit in your chest. The right lung is a little larger than the left lung because the left lung has to share its space with the heart.

HOW MANY BREATHS TO FILL?

Number of breaths

30,000,000	High-altitude airship: **29,449,520**
28,000,000	
26,000,000	
24,000,000	
22,000,000	
20,000,000	
18,000,000	
16,000,000	Hot-air balloon: **14,724,760**
14,000,000	
12,000,000	
10,000,000	
8,000,000	
6,000,000	
4,000,000	
2,000,000	Blimp: **1,147,965**
4	Party balloon: **4**
1	Lungs: **1**
0	

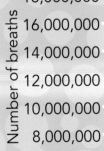

BREATHS

You normally breathe in **17 ounces** (500 ml) of air with each breath. When you sleep you require less oxygen than when you are running around or playing a sport. When resting, the average adult takes around **12 to 20 breaths per minute**. If you breathe **20 times a minute**, you have breathed in **2.6 gallons** (10 liters) of air.

Number of breaths:
One hour: 1,200
Six hours: 7,200
12 hours: 14,400
24 hours: 28,800

Humans breathe in between **2,300 and 3,800 gallons** (8,640 and 14,400 liters) **of air** each day.

ALVEOLI

An average adult's lungs can contain around **480,000,000 alveoli**.

When you breathe in, the air travels down through your nose or mouth, down through your throat, and into your windpipe.

The windpipe splits into two smaller tubes: one goes to the left lung and the other to the right lung.

The inside of your lungs is like a giant sponge, filled with a mass of tubes. The tubes from the windpipe divide an additional **15 to 25 times** into thousands of smaller airways that eventually lead to tiny air sacs, called alveoli.

Lungs expand and contract—like filling a balloon with air and then deflating it.

You have muscles that help you breathe, such as your diaphragm, which sits beneath the lungs. When you breathe in, your breathing muscles contract, pulling your ribs up and out. The space within your chest increases and air flows into your lungs. When you breathe out, your muscles relax and your ribs move down and in. The space within your chest decreases and air flows out.

MORE THAN SIX HUNDRED MUSCLES IN YOUR BODY

All movement in the body is powered by your muscles.
Different sources group muscles differently, so it is difficult to state the exact number of muscles in the human body. All sources agree that the number of muscles is above **600**; some sources have categorized as many as **850 muscles** in the body.

THERE ARE THREE TYPES OF MUSCLE

Skeletal muscles
These muscles are attached to bones and help them move. They are areas of stretchy tissue, built up in layers.

Cardiac muscle
This is the muscle that the heart is made of.

Smooth muscles
These are found in the walls of your internal organs, such as the arteries that carry the blood around your body.

40% of your body weight is made up of muscle.

Some muscles are involuntary. They work without thinking, like your heart beating. Other muscles are voluntary. They are controlled by your thoughts and allow you to move things around, including yourself.

It takes **43 muscles** to frown but only **17 muscles** to smile.

HOW THEY WORK

Muscles work by expanding and contracting. When the biceps contract, the triceps relax, which allows your arm to bend. When you straighten your arm back out, the biceps will relax and the triceps will contract.

Many of your muscles come in pairs, like the biceps and triceps. Muscle pairs allow you to move parts of your body back and forth.

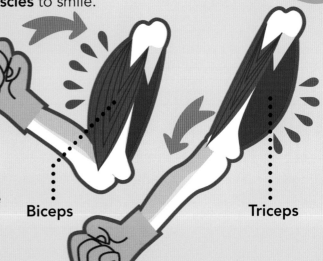

Biceps

Triceps

IMPORTANT MUSCLES AND HOW THEY HELP US

Abdominal muscles help support your body when it's upright.

The shortest and smallest muscle is in your ears and is the **stapedius**. It is attached to the smallest bone in the body, the stapes. At around **0.05 inches** (1.27 mm), this muscle helps conduct sound vibrations, which allow you to hear.

Pectoralis muscles help you pull and push objects.

The hardest-working muscle is the **heart**. It performs the most physical work in the course of a lifetime.

Biceps and triceps help you lift up objects.

The largest muscle is the **gluteus maximus**, which makes up part of your buttocks.

The longest muscle in the human body is the **sartorius**. It runs from the hip to the knee on the inside of the leg and helps you bend your knee and twist your leg. This muscle can be as long as **24 inches** (60 cm).

Quadriceps help you lift up your knee.

Calf muscles help you walk, run, and jump.

EXERCISE

When you exercise, you work your muscles, which allows them to become bigger and stronger. But don't just focus on building muscles. If you have too much muscle bulk, your movement may become restricted, and you could become short of breath, putting a strain on your heart. It's important to perform aerobic exercise, such as running, which will keep your heart healthy.

RECOMMENDED LEVELS OF EXERCISE FOR ADULTS, PER WEEK:

Two hours and 30 minutes
Moderate aerobic activity, such as cycling or fast walking, and muscle-strengthening activities on two or more days a week.
Or
One hour and 15 minutes
Intensive aerobic activity, such as running or a game of tennis.
And muscle-strengthening activities on two or more days a week.
Muscle-strengthening activities could include lifting weights, yoga, or even gardening.

206 BONES IN THE HUMAN BODY

350

206

The skeleton is a framework of bones.
It holds your body up, protects vital organs, and has joints attached to muscles that allow you to move.

When we are babies, we have **350 bones** in our bodies. As we grow, some bones join together and we end up with **206 bones** by the time we reach adulthood.

WHAT ARE BONES MADE OF?
Bones are made up of layers of hard tissue that have a spongy inner layer that surrounds soft tissue called bone marrow. Bone marrow is where blood cells are made. The cells leave the bone through tiny holes.

STRONG AND LIGHT
Bones are strong enough to support your weight but also light enough to allow movement.

Actual size ••••

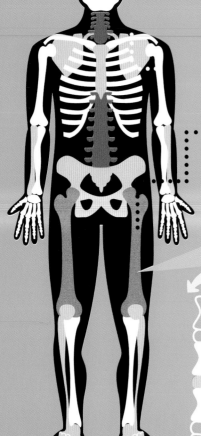

The stape, which is inside your ear, is the smallest bone in your body, measuring **0.12 inches** (3mm). •••

The thigh bone, also known as the femur, is the longest, largest, and strongest bone in your body. The femur is **26%** of a person's height.

VERTEBRAL COLUMN
The vertebral column is also known as the backbone, or spine. It is a column of **24 individual bones** called vertebrae. The column extends from the base of the skull down to the bottom of the back. Each vertebra is connected by joints, similar to a tiny ball and socket joint. The joints are surrounded by rubbery tissue called cartilage that cushions the movement of the bones.

206 BONES

Hands: **54**

Feet: **52**

Thorax: **25**

Vertebral column: **24**

Facial bones: **14**

Head: **8**

Legs: **8**

Middle ears: **6**

Arms: **6**

Shoulders: **4**

Pelvis: **4**

Throat: **1**

FRACTURES

A fracture is the medical term for a broken bone. Fractures can take **three to 10 weeks** to heal. The younger you are, the quicker they are likely to mend.

There are many different types of fractures, depending on the kind of break and injury to the bone. Here are **eight** different types:

TRANSVERSE

OBLIQUE

SPIRAL

COMMINUTED

AVULSION

IMPACTED

TORUS

GREENSTICK

TEETH

Teeth are part of the skeletal structure but are not counted as bones because they are made of different material.

12-72 HOURS TO DIGEST FOOD

Food provides you with the fuel your body needs to grow and the energy your body needs so that you can move. When you eat food, it travels through your body in the digestive system. This system is made up of a series of organs that extract nutrients from food. The food that your body doesn't need comes out of the anus as feces, or poop.

JOURNEY TIME

Food can take between **12 and 72 hours** to travel through the digestive system. This is largely based on the type of food you have eaten. Foods that are rich in fiber, such as fruit, will travel through the digestive system quickly, whereas foods such as red meat take much longer to break down into waste matter.

SALIVA

You produce **34 to 51 ounces** (1 to 1.5 liters) of saliva every day.

2% enzymes
98% water

Saliva is mostly water, but it contains a small percentage of enzymes. Enzymes are digestive juices that break down food into tiny pieces.

Food takes up to **eight seconds** to travel down the esophagus into the stomach.

12 hours

72 hours

Feces
The average human will produce around **360 pounds** (163.29 kg) of feces a year. That's just under **1 pound** (450 g) of feces in a day.

Feces is made up of:

- 75% water
- 8% indigestible fibers
- 8% dead bacteria
- 4% fats
- 4% salts
- 1% protein

THE STOMACH

contains acid. Along with the stomach walls, the acid breaks the food into tiny pieces. Good bacteria in the stomach attack any harmful bacteria that may have traveled down.

THE ACID

in the stomach means that the stomach has to replace its lining every **three to four days**. That's between **91 to 122 stomach linings** a year.

THE LIVER

has over **500 different functions** that help your body. Within the digestive system it releases a yellowish-brown fluid, called bile, which helps to break down fats within food.

THE PANCREAS

releases enzymes that break down the food into even tinier pieces and help absorb nutrients from the food.

THE SMALL INTESTINE

absorbs all the remaining nutrients from the food. These nutrients pass through the intestine's lining into your blood, which then circulates around your body. These nutrients are important for the growth of your cells.

THE LARGE INTESTINE

converts food waste into feces.

THE INTESTINES

The small intestine is about **20 feet** (6 m) long. It's almost **four times** as long as the average adult is tall. The large intestine is **5 feet** (1.5 m) long.

They are so named because the diameter of the small intestine is much smaller than that of the large intestine.

NINE MONTHS FOR A BABY TO GROW INSIDE THE WOMB

Between the ages of 9 and 15, the female body goes through a period called puberty. During this time, the body goes through changes that make it possible for women to conceive and have babies.

PREGNANCY

A baby starts to grow after its mother's egg joins with its father's sperm. It takes approximately **nine months** for a baby to grow until it is ready to be born. The period of time inside the womb is called pregnancy. During the pregnancy, the baby will develop all of its limbs and internal organs.

A baby's heart will beat **54,000,000** times before birth.

TAKING SHAPE

As the baby grows within the womb, its different body organs begin to take shape at different times.

Week 1

Week 6: arms and legs start to take shape.

Week 8: lungs, ears, and eyes start to form. The developing baby is now called a fetus.

Week 9: fingers and toes are defined.

Week 14: nose, lips, and taste buds are formed.

Week 25: hair has recognizable color and texture.

Weeks 35–40: the baby is usually born during this period.

SIZE OF BABY IN THE WOMB AS FRUIT

WEIGHT OF BABY

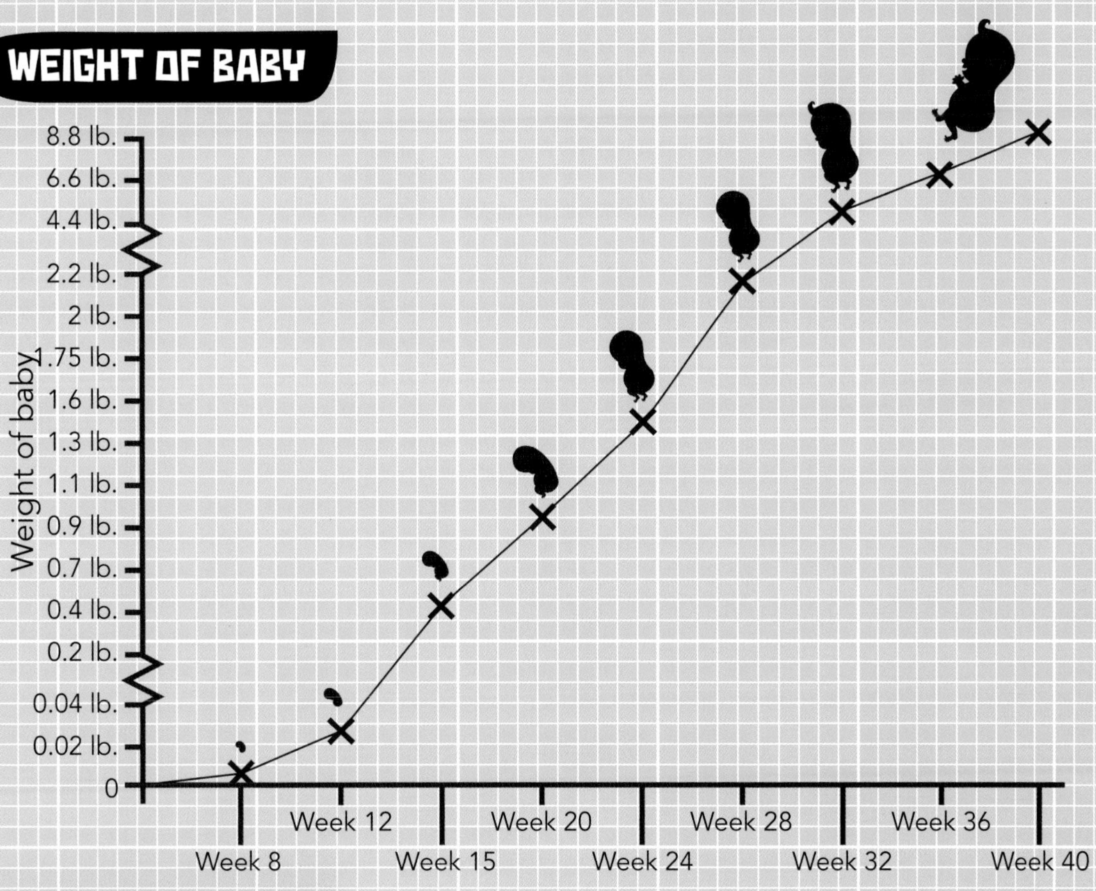

8.8 lb.
6.6 lb.
4.4 lb.
2.2 lb.
2 lb.
1.75 lb.
1.6 lb.
1.3 lb.
1.1 lb.
0.9 lb.
0.7 lb.
0.4 lb.
0.2 lb.
0.04 lb.
0.02 lb.
0
Weight of baby
Week 8
Week 12
Week 15
Week 20
Week 24
Week 28
Week 32
Week 36
Week 40

HEIGHT OF BABY

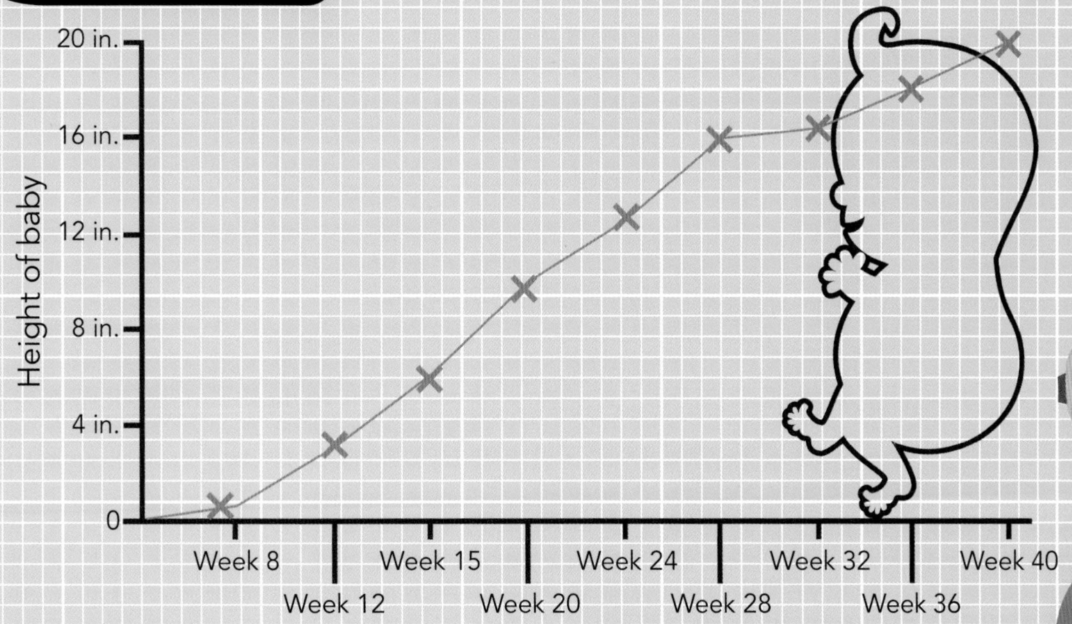

20 in.
16 in.
12 in.
8 in.
4 in.
0
Height of baby
Week 8
Week 12
Week 15
Week 20
Week 24
Week 28
Week 32
Week 36
Week 40

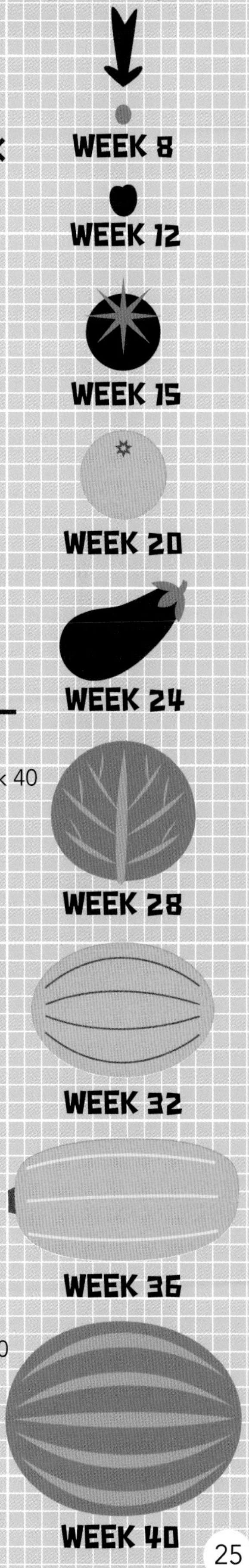

WEEK 8
WEEK 12
WEEK 15
WEEK 20
WEEK 24
WEEK 28
WEEK 32
WEEK 36
WEEK 40

FIVE SENSES

The human body has five sense organs that gather information on the world around you.

YOUR TONGUE is covered with **2,000** to **10,000** tiny **bumps** called taste buds. When you are young, you have more taste buds; they become weaker and die out as you get older.

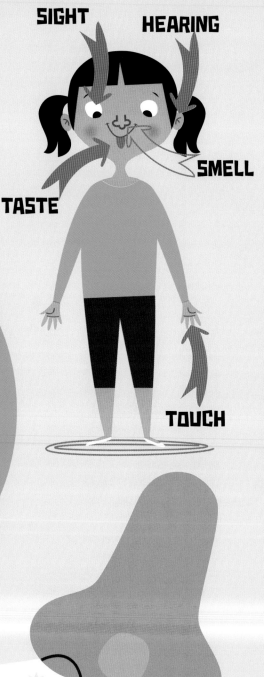

YOUR TASTE BUDS DETECT FIVE MAIN TASTES!

UMAMI

SOUR

BITTER

SWEET

SALTY

The taste buds that recognize these flavors are spread over the tongue in different densities.

YOUR NOSE breathes in particles from the air and is able to pick out smells that they contain.

The average person's nose can detect more than **10,000 different smells**. When you have a stuffy nose, food may have little or no taste. This is because your sense of smell works with the sense of taste to detect the flavor of food. Your sense of smell is much stronger than your sense of taste. Approximately **80%** of what we taste is understood through our sense of smell.

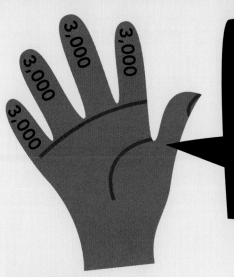

TOUCH

You have cells, called receptors, that are near the surface of your skin. These receptors are able to detect pain, pressure, touch, and temperature. They are able to tell you whether an object is hard or soft, hot or cold, sharp or blunt. There are about **3,000 touch receptors** in each of your fingers.

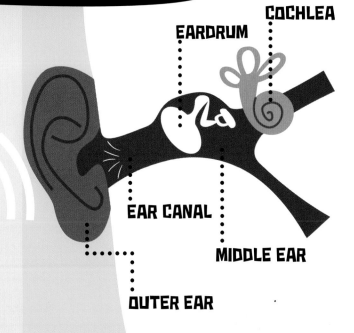

EARDRUM

COCHLEA

EAR CANAL

MIDDLE EAR

OUTER EAR

HEARING

Sound travels through the air in sound waves. Your outer ear catches the sound waves, and they travel into the ear canal. Their vibrations are felt on the eardrum and against tiny hairs. These sensations travel to the brain where the waves are translated into the sounds that we hear. We have approximately **15,000 hair cells** in each ear.

  + = **30,000 hair cells** in your ears.

SIGHT

Light bounces off objects and enters your eye through the pupil. A lens in the eye focuses the light on the retina at the back of the eyeball. Light sensitive cells in the retina pick up the image, but it is upside down. This image is sent to your brain, which turns it the right way around.

Your pupils widen and narrow to let in different amounts of light.

When it is dark, your pupils widen to let in more light so that you can see more.

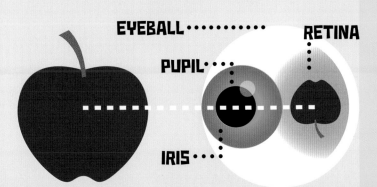

EYEBALL

RETINA

PUPIL

IRIS

THE HUMAN BRAIN WEIGHS 3 POUNDS

Your senses send information to the brain through the nervous system. The brain translates this information into the smells, sights, sounds, tastes, and physical sensations that we recognize.

THE NERVOUS SYSTEM

Your brain and spinal cord form the main components of the central nervous system. Together they act as your body's control center. The spinal cord is a long, thin cable of nerve fibers. It gathers together the pathways of nerves that run through your body, connecting to every organ and muscle. It is the channel for carrying messages from these nerves to and from your brain.

THE BRAIN

The brain sits inside your skull. The brain is the place where thoughts, emotions, and memories are processed. It controls your movement, skills, and the functions necessary to live. It is made up of over **100,000,000,000 nerve cells**. Nerve cells in the brain are also known as neurons. You could fit **30,000 neurons** on the head of a pin. You would need over **33,333,333 pinheads** to contain all of the brain's neurons.

The brain also contains over **400 miles** (643 km) of blood vessels. That's the same distance from London to Edinburgh, or from Boston, Massachusetts, to Washington, D.C.

BOSTON

WASHINGTON, D.C.

The brain is a jellylike mass of ridges and grooves.

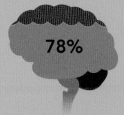

78%

Approximately **78%** of your brain is water.

AVERAGE BRAIN SIZE:

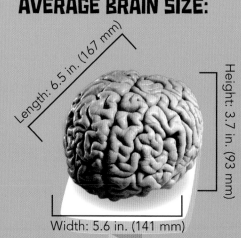

Length: 6.5 in. (167 mm)

Height: 3.7 in. (93 mm)

Width: 5.6 in. (141 mm)

Weight: 3 lb. (1.4 kg)

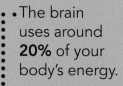

The brain is only about **2%** of your body weight.

The brain uses around **20%** of your body's energy.

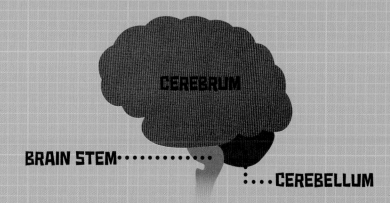

CEREBRUM

BRAIN STEM

CEREBELLUM

THE BRAIN IS MADE OF THREE MAIN PARTS

The cerebrum is the largest part of the human brain. It's the area that allows you to think, understand sensory perceptions, and store memories.

The cerebellum controls your balance and tells your muscles how to move.

The brain stem connects the brain to the spinal cord. It controls the involuntary muscles that work without you thinking, for example, the internal organs, such as the heart, lungs, and stomach.

Two sides of the brain

The cerebrum is divided down the middle into a right hemisphere and a left hemisphere. Each hemisphere appears to be specialized for some behaviors. The right side of the brain controls muscles on the left side of the body, and the left side of the brain controls muscles on the right side of the body.

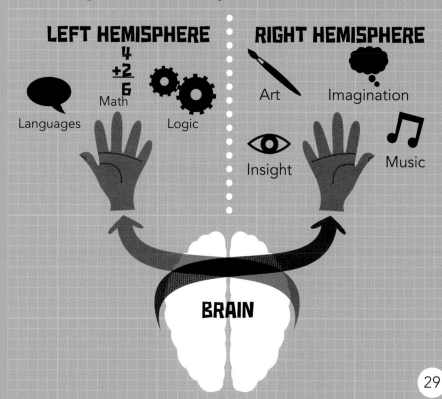

LEFT HEMISPHERE

Math

Logic

Languages

RIGHT HEMISPHERE

Art

Imagination

Insight

Music

BRAIN

FURTHER INFORMATION

BOOKS

Essential Life Science: The Human Body by Melanie Waldron (Heinemann Library, 2014)
Project Science: The Human Body by Sally Hewitt (Franklin Watts, 2013)
Superscience: Human Body by Rob Colson (Franklin Watts, 2013)
The World in Infographics: The Human Body by Jon Richards (Owlkids Books, 2013)

WEBSITES

Interactive site with videos and fun facts:
http://easyscienceforkids.com/human-body/
Videos, quizzes, and word searches covering all parts of the human body:
http://kidshealth.org/kid/htbw/
Short videos, text, and images covering the different systems of the human body:
www.kidsbiology.com/human_biology/

Note to parents and teachers:
Every effort has been made by the publisher to ensure that these websites contain no inappropriate or offensive material. However, because of the nature of the Internet, it is impossible to guarantee that the content of these sites will not be altered. We strongly advise that Internet access is supervised by a responsible adult.

LARGE NUMBERS

1,000,000,000,000,000,000,000,000,000,000,000 = ONE DECILLION

1,000,000,000,000,000,000,000,000,000,000 = ONE NONILLION

1,000,000,000,000,000,000,000,000,000 = ONE OCTILLION

1,000,000,000,000,000,000,000,000 = ONE SEPTILLION

1,000,000,000,000,000,000,000 = ONE SEXTILLION

1,000,000,000,000,000,000 = ONE QUINTILLION

1,000,000,000,000,000 = ONE QUADRILLION

1,000,000,000,000 = ONE TRILLION

1,000,000,000 = ONE BILLION

1,000,000 = ONE MILLION

1,000 = ONE THOUSAND

100 = ONE HUNDRED

10 = TEN

1 = ONE

GLOSSARY

anatomy	the scientific study of the bodily structures of humans, animals, and plants
average	the usual amount or an estimated or calculated means of division to find the middle number of a set
bacteria	a single-cell organism that can be found in animals, plants, earth, water, and in the air
bald	an area on the body not covered with hair
carbon dioxide	a gas produced when people and animals breathe out
cell	a small element of a living organism
circulation	a movement that is circular or flows through a circuit
digestive system	a system of organs responsible for getting food in and out of your body and extracting valuable nutrients for your body's health
dissection	to cut apart in order to examine a structure
enzymes	proteins that perform chemical changes in the body
fiber	food matter that cannot be digested but helps the digestion of other food
follicle	a tiny hole in the skin from where a hair grows
fracture	a crack or break in a bone
genetic	an inherited biological characteristic
glands	a group of cells or organs that combine and release substances around the body
infection	a disease caused by germs that enter the body
keratin	a protein substance that is found in hair and nails
melanin	a pigment that gives color to skin and hair
microorganisms	organisms, such as bacteria, that are too small to be seen with the naked eye
microscope	an instrument that uses lenses to magnify the image of small objects
muscles	body tissues made up of fibers that move the different parts of your body
nervous system	a system where your brain sends and receives messages through a network of nerves around your body to control movement and feeling
neurons	cells that carry messages between the brain and other parts of the body
nutrients	substances that are beneficial to growth and well-being
organism	a living thing that is able to function independently
oxygen	a gas that people and animals breathe in, which is necessary for life
plasma	the watery part of blood that contains blood cells
puberty	a period of growth during which a child's body develops into an adult's body and is capable of sexual reproduction
respiratory system	the system in which the body breathes in oxygen and breathes out carbon dioxide
saliva	watery fluid that gets released in the mouth and aids digestion
tissue	a collection of cells that have a similar structure and function
umami	a taste sensation that is savory and meaty
vessels	veins or arteries that carry blood through the body

INDEX